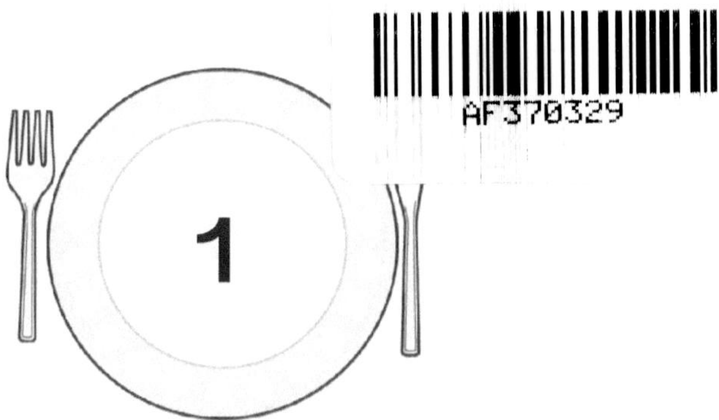

The word "gastronomy" was created in 1801 by Joseph Berchoux, French poet and humorist. Etymologically, "gastro" means "stomach" and "nomos" means "rule"; gastronomy is the set of rules that define the art of cooking well, and eating well together.

The first gastronomy of a country classified as an intangible cultural heritage of humanity is France, in 2010 — or more precisely "the gastronomic meal of French people". According to UNESCO experts indeed, French cuisine strengthens collective identity of the country and contributes to the world cultural diversity. In 2013, traditional Mexican cuisine, Mediterranean diet, and washoku (Japanese New Year's menu) were added.

Sugar consumption has literally exploded around the world: +46% over the last 30 years. Sugar lobbies (American beverage association, American sugar alliance, Coca-Cola…), who spend massively to influence public authorities to their advantage, are surely not innocent in this situation.

It all started in 1964 when the Sugar Research Foundation paid scientists to explain saturated fats (not sugar) were increasing the risk of heart disease; multiple studies have now demonstrated the role of sugar in cardiovascular diseases.

Since then, sugar lobbies have been very active: more than €20 million spent each year in Europe to influence the European Commission decisions, and between $30 and 50 million in the United States.

All edible oils do not remain stable at the same temperatures. Beyond a certain threshold (called the smoke point), they burn, decompose and denature, and release toxic substances sometimes carcinogenic. For example, palm oil burns at 240°C/464°F, extra virgin olive oil at 191°C/376°F, butter at 177°C/351°F, and flaxseed oil at 107°C/225°F.

Refined oils have more neutral flavors and limited nutritional benefits, but a higher smoke point than virgin and extra virgin oils.

Thus, for frying it is preferred to use oils with a high smoke point capable of enduring higher temperatures and making possible to obtain crispy foods. For salads dressing, extra virgin oils rich in mono and poly-unsaturated fats are recommended.

On average, Americans spend around 9.5% of their income on food, half of it consumed at home and the other half away from home. It was nearly 17% in 1960. In France, the proportion of food spending at home went down from 30% in the 1950s to 15% today.

According to Engel's law, the higher the share of income is allocated to food, the lower the income. This is verifiable in real life, for example in France the 10% of households with the lowest standard of living spend 18% of their budget on food, while this share is around 14% for the 10% with the highest standard of living.

We also see this correlation at the country level, Switzerland allocating only 6% of their income to food at home, while it is almost 50% of it in Pakistan.

The term "microbiota" refers to all bacteria, archaea, protists, fungi and viruses that coexist with humans. The largest amounts of bacteria are found in the digestive tract: more than 10 billion are located in the colon. If several hundreds of different species exist, the two dominant groups are called firmicutes and bacteroids.

Gut microbiota helps break down food components that humans cannot digest such as starch, plant fibers, and certain vitamins. Considered as our second brain, it is unique to everyone. Moreover, its bacterial population evolves over the course of life depending on the type of food eaten and antibiotic usage.

It is largely admitted the microbiome could be the key to treat all sorts of diseases.

Besides their exceptional banquets, the Romans only had one real full meal a day – dinner – which was taken around 3pm. Breakfast consisted of water and a bit of bread, and lunch was optional. At that time, meals were a place of great negotiations.

The 3 meals at fixed times appeared with the rise of Fordism at the beginning of the 20th century: the workers had to respect a precise schedule with a single break at noon, and it was forbidden to eat on the production line. So they ate before work, at midday and after work on their way home.

Nowadays, these fixed-time meals are fading in many countries even if they are still the norm.

Foie gras history begins in ancient Egypt over 4,500 years ago with the invention of the force-feeding technique on birds in order to fatten them up.

The consumption of foie gras as it is understood today began in ancient Rome, in the south-west of Gaul, where Romans perfected it. Today, France is the largest producer (75% of the 25,000 tons produced in the world) and consumer of foie gras (660g per household per year).

Due to controversy over force-feeding, several associations campaigning for animal welfare are putting pressure; several countries and states have thus promulgated laws against the production and / or marketing of foie gras.

Fasting was a tool practiced to rebalance the body before our era, and was encouraged as early as the 1st century BC. This practice only began to be considered excessive in the 1600s. It is nowadays dispensed for religious, ritual, ethical or health reasons. Many specialists have indeed shown its properties for the organism, in particular detoxifying and therapeutic.

There are 2 main types of fasting: intermittent fasting is a short, discontinuous fast, with a certain frequency; the best known are the 16/8 (16h of fasting each day) and the 5/2 (2 days per week). Continuous fasting is longer but episodic (for example for a week twice a year).

What gives fruits and vegetables their colors is their pigments content:

- Chlorophyll brings a green color (basil, cabbage).
- Carotene (family of carotenoids) gives a red, orange or yellow color (carrot).
- Flavonoids give a yellow tint when cooked in water (spinach).
- Anthocyanins provide a purple, blue or red coloring depending on the PH level (beet, red cabbage, grapes).

These natural pigments, which are part of the family of polyphenols, have antioxidant effects. They lose their properties in contact with heat and air.

In English language, we use an Italian word to refer to "pasta". The word "spaghetti" on the other hand comes from Arabic language, and means "thread" or "string".

Arabs were actually the first to have the idea of hanging noodles on clotheslines to dry them, and thus be able to keep them longer. This technique was introduced in Italy at the time of the conquest of Sicily by the Arabs, and then spread throughout Europe.

Today, there are no less than 350 different shapes of pasta around the world – from which Pappardelle, Orecchiette, Macaroni, Linguine, Farfalle, Fusilli, Fettuccine, and Capellini, just to name a few.

"Real" pasta, since 1547, are made from only 3 ingredients: durum wheat flour, salt and water.

Bangladesh is the country where people consume the least meat per capita over the world: only about 4kg per year. Next come India, Burundi, Sri Lanka, and African countries such as Rwanda, Sierra Leone, Eritrea, Mozambique, Gambia, and Malawi.

At the other end of the spectrum are the United States with inhabitants eating more than 100kg of meat per year per person… which is almost 30 times more! Kuwait and Australia are the two countries completing the podium of the biggest meat eaters.

As for Western Europeans, they consume between 80 and 90kg of meat per person and per year depending on the country.

The average person in the world consumed around 45kg of meat – pork being the popular and poultry the fastest growing.

815 million people worldwide suffer from hunger, and 9 million people die each year from malnutrition (including 3 million children under the age of 5). Paradoxically, today more than half the production of barley, millet, oats and corn is used to feed livestock.

While these deaths mainly occur in countries suffering from extreme poverty, all countries over the world are confronted with a form of malnutrition: children growth retardation, anemia in woman of childbearing age, people In overweight.

Globally, 2 billion people suffer from deficiencies in essential micronutrients, such as iron, vitamin A or iodine. Iron deficiency is actually the most common and widespread nutritional disorder in the world.

Botanical classification of fruits and vegetables depends on their edible part:

- Root vegetables: carrot, celeriac, turnip, radish.
- Tubers: potato.
- Bulb vegetables: fennel, onion, garlic, shallot, leek, celery stalk.
- Leaf vegetables: salad, spinach, chard, white cabbage, green, red.
- Inflorescence vegetables: broccoli, cauliflower, Brussels sprouts, artichoke.
- Vegetable-fruits: cucumber, tomato, pepper, squash, zucchini, eggplant, pickle, pumpkin.
- Pods: green beans, peas.
- Rhizomes: Jerusalem artichoke, asparagus.

Proteins help to build, repair and maintain muscles. Since the body cannot store them, they must be consumed regularly — via plants and / or via animals.

In order to meet basic nutritional requirements, proteins should represent between 10 and 15% of the daily food intake, or in other words about 0.8g of protein per kilo of body weight. It therefore represents 60g of protein per day for a 75kg man (equivalent of 240g of steak), and 40g of protein for a 50kg woman (equivalent of 160g of steak).

In the Western world today, two-thirds of the proteins consumed come from of animals (meat, fish, crustaceans, eggs) and one-third from plants (cereals, legumes, soybeans).

Vegetarianism began between 600 and 500 BC in the Indus Valley, even if at the time the word does not exist. The reason for this emergence is based on the development of a religion based on non-violence towards all living beings – an early form of Hinduism.

Hinduism is nowadays the third most widely practiced religion in the world with around 750 million followers; it prohibits the consumption of any animal because of reincarnation which could make us cannibals. Nowadays, many Indians consider Hinduism, the native religion of India, to be more of a way of life and culture than a religion.

Buddhism, Sikhism, and Jainism also believe that no life should be voluntarily destroyed for human gratification.

Oranges belong to a large group of fruits known as citrus fruits. If their cultivation seems to have started in eastern Asia (probably in China) thousands of years ago, nowadays they are grown in most warm regions of the world. The total production of oranges is about 70 million tons.

The world's largest producer of orange is Brazil (almost one third of the world's output), then comes the United States (10%), Mexico, India, China, Spain, Egypt and Italy.

Among the most popular orange varieties are the Valencia (the "summer" orange), the Navel (the "winter" orange), and the tangerine.

The first frozen food appeared on the market in the 1930s, at first on seafood products, thanks to the American Clarence Birdseye.

Deep-freezing is an industrial method using extremely low temperatures to cool the food very quickly. Thus, in addition to a very long conservation, most nutritional and organoleptic qualities are maintained, especially over a short storage time and if the food is well packaged.

Home-freezing also blocks microbial development, and therefore extends products shelf life. However, as their temperature drops slowly, it does not guarantee the same food safety and causes crystals that break food cells, emptying them from their content during defrosting.

The first warning against sugar appeared in 1709 by the French doctor Philippe Hecquet.

Americans are today the population easting the most sugar in the world: 46kg per year, which corresponds to almost 130g per person and per day. It is more than Germans (37kg per year, 101g per day), French (35kg per year, 96g per day), Australians (35kg per year, 95g per day), English people (34kg per year, 93g per day), Canada (32kg per year, 89g per day)… and much more than Indians (18.5kg per year, 50g per day).

The WHO (World Health Organization) estimates that sugar should not exceed 10% of our total daily energy intake, which represents about 22g of sugar per day per person (9kg / year). The ideal recommended by the WHO is even 5% – or about 11g daily.

The first hotels appeared in Greece from the 4th century BC. They enable citizens to no longer have to provide hospitality to foreigners. These basic comfort hotels also served as taverns. The word "hotel" appeared in Europe from the 12th century, and it was not until the 14th century that they began to offer lockable single rooms.

The term "restaurant", which first refers to a thick broth, was then given to the places where they were served. The first restaurants, which appeared in Paris in the 1780s, were hostels for the wealthy. One of them, "Le Procope", quickly became an institution.

The palace was created in the 1890s by César Ritz.

Among nobles, from the 1740s, a meal did not aim to satisfy needs (to be satiated), but gluttony. In the 19th century, a distinction appeared in France between "gourmandize" (considered as quality) and gluttony (weakness).

Nowadays, food that has become desire is not satisfactory without this dimension of "pleasure" and fulfillment in terms of emotions and sensations.

However, some doctrines consider gourmandize as a defect. In Abrahamic religions, it is opposed to the teachings of moderation. In the Christian religion, gourmandize is one of the seven deadly sins. Furthermore, the first principle of Greek dietetics as well as Chinese medicine and Ayurveda is moderation.

In 1538, the Spanish explorer Piedro Cieza de Leon discovered the potato in Peru, where it was called "papas". It appeared in Europe in the 1570s — first in Spain under the name of "patata", then in Italy where it was called "taratouffli"; yet, it only became popular 30 years later.

Today, there are around 500 varieties of potatoes in the world, but only 80 of them are grown commercially. Potatoes can be classified into 7 categories:
- Russet potatoes (rough brown skin).
- Red potatoes.
- White potatoes.
- Yellow potatoes (also called Yukon potatoes).
- Purple/blue potatoes.
- Fingerling.
- Petite.

When a knife blade slices an onion, an enzyme from the onion (called alliinase) is released. In contact with air, it leads to the formation of a volatile tear gas compound. When this gas comes in contact with the liquid protecting our eyes from dust, it dissolves; this leads to the formation of particularly irritating sulfuric acid, which causes itching. Tears are thus produced abundantly to rinse the eyes.

Placing the onion under a stream of water during cutting stops the diffusion of the gas since it is dissolved by water. Another tip is to cut the onion in a plastic bag, which will stop the enzymes released into the air, or to protect your eyes with diving goggles.

The word "soda" used to talk about carbonated beverage refers to soda ash that makes possible to obtain carbon dioxide. Those carbonated drinks contain, depending on the case, fruit extracts, sugar, additives (flavors, colors, preservatives, benzoic and ascorbic acids...).

The first soda was created in 1793 by a watchmaker (Johann Jacob Schweppe): Schweppe water. It was intended for medical use and prescribed to treat illness of the kidneys and gallbladder, indigestion and gout. "Soda water" term was only used from 1798.

The current world's top three countries in terms of soda sales are Mexico (147 liters per capita), Chile (144 liters) and the United States (126 liters).

BMI (Body Mass Index) was invented in 1858 by a Belgian mathematician and statistician in order to measure the "normality" of weight. It is calculated simply by dividing the weight (in kg) by the square of the height (in meters).

A normal BMI is between 18.5 and 25. Below 18.5 is anorexia, beyond 25 overweight, beyond 30 obesity and beyond 40 morbid obesity.

Other methods exist to define the ideal weight. For example the Lorentz formula below determine the ideal weight according to the sex:

- Men: Size – 100 – [(size – 150) / 4]
- Women: Size – 100 – [(size – 150) / 2.5]

(size in centimeters)

Phosphate, along with nitrogen and potassium, is one of the essential elements for a plant to grow. Derived from phosphorus, this natural mineral substance is now mainly used as a natural or chemical fertilizer.

Phosphate has started to be used to feed the soil in the middle of the 19th century in order to increase the production of cereals, and thus avoid famines. The first nitrogen and potassium fertilizer factory opened in 1838 in Valenciennes, France.

Nowadays, massive use of fertilizers has important consequences on both the environment and humans health with consequences such as air and river pollution, soil depletion, erosion, proliferation of green algae, global warming.

Margherita pizza was invented in 1889 by the Italian Raffaele Esposito in honor of the Queen of Italy Marguerite of Savoy. It was a pizza with tomatoes, mozzarella and basil: this pizza was actually representing the Italian flag.

Today, nearly 30 billion pizzas are consumed worldwide each year. The United States is the largest consumer and accounts for about 10% of the total world consumption.

It is also in the United States that can be found the most expensive pizza of the world, in a restaurant in New York. It is made up of 4 kinds of caviar, lobster tail, salmon eggs, wasabi and crème fraîche… And is sold US $ 1,000!

Natural flavors can be produced using different techniques, either alone or combined depending on the aroma profile targeted:

- Concentration: elimination of water to obtain a dehydrated product or an aqueous concentrate (for example an orange concentrate).
- Distillation: separation of mixtures by evaporation then condensation (essential oil).
- Extraction: chemical separation of a compound using a solvent.
- Maceration.
- Infusion (hot extraction).

Whatever the technique used, the aroma concentration phenomenon also concentrates, at once, pollutants.

Nearly one-third of the European Union inhabitants are not eating fruits and vegetables on a daily basis. Among the other two-third, around 75% are consuming between one and four portions of fruit and vegetables each day and 25% five or more.

There are important discrepancies among countries, from those consuming little quantities (Greece, Slovenia, Austria, Croatia, Bulgaria and Romania) to the bigger consumers (Italy, the United Kingdom, the Netherlands, Denmark, Ireland, Portugal and Belgium). More than half of the population in Bulgaria and Romania don't include fruits and vegetables in their daily diet.

Both the WHO and the FAO recommend adults to consume at least five servings of fruits and vegetables per day (or 400g).

The principle of whipping egg whites into what is called "snow" was created in the 6th century by the Byzantine doctor Anthime. This invention is mentioned in his book "De observatione ciborum", a dietetic treatise in which there are many cooking recipes.

However, it was not until the Renaissance that it became a sweet treat with the invention of "snow egg".

In 2014, vegetable snow egg was invented when Frenchman Joël Roessel, in his blog "Vegetal revolution", replaced egg white with chickpea juice. The word "aquafaba" (bean water) was created the following year to refer to this liquid.

It is today widely used in vegetarian and vegan cuisines.

At the end of the 19th century, Nicolas Appert developed a method of preserving food: canning. He was motivated by the 12,000 francs offered at that time by Napoléon to any inventor who could develop a cheap and effective method of preserving food.

This technique consists in subjecting a sufficiently intense heat treatment to a perishable food so that it ensures its long-term stability, even at room temperature. The process involves the use of sealed containers (first tin cans, then metal, glass jars).

The world's first canning factory was created by Nicolas Appert in 1795 in France. The use of what is known today as "canned goods" developed and became widespread after the Second World War.

Vitamin C, also called ascorbic acid, is found in many food products. It is a natural antioxidant widely used in the food industry as a preservative.

Since vitamin C is hardly stored in the body, a daily food intake is necessary. The main sources of vitamin C are raw fruits and vegetables (vitamin C being particularly heat-sensitive), especially kiwis, citrus fruits, red peppers, broccoli, spinach and cabbage. If vitamin C exists in supplements, most experts recommend getting it from fruits and vegetables as it is better absorbed by our organism.

Smokers have an increased need for vitamin C because in this case it is used to neutralize some chemicals produced during the combustion of tobacco.

The link between health and food started to be made in ancient Greece. According to Hippocrates, the founder of modern medicine, the human body has an innate capacity for self-healing, and nutrition helps maintain a good health. "Let your food be your medicine, and your medicine, your food," he proclaimed 400 years before Christ. Today, numerous studies confirm that diet accounts for at least 80% of our health.

Hu Zheng Qi Huei, a Mongolian imperial dietitian, was he first who described deficiency-related illnesses and their treatment with diet. His book, "Important Principles of Food and Drink", is a classic in Chinese medicine and cuisine.

The chewing-gum was created in 1848 in the United States by John Bacon Curtis, and popularized in Europe by the Americans at the end of the First World War.

Many kinds of gums and pastes were already chewed in prehistoric times: coniferous sap, chews made from birch sap, or even sap from sapodilla. Asians chewed betel, Indians of the Andes chewed the nuts of kola tree, and Indians of the Amazon the nuts of tobacco balls.

Today, 374 billion chewing-gums are consumed worldwide each year; Americans are the biggest consumers, followed by French. It has been banned in Singapore since 1992.

Western vegetarianism excludes the consumption of meat, fish and shellfish (all animal flesh), but allows eggs and dairy products. In contrast, Indian vegetarianism (which actually saw vegetarianism rise through religion) authorizes the consumption of dairy products, but excludes eggs and mushrooms.

Lacto-vegetarianism excludes all animal products except dairy products, ovo-vegetarianism excludes all animal products except eggs, pesco-vegetarianism excludes all animal products except fish.

As for veganism, all products "using" animals are excluded: honey, gelatin, meat broth, butter, leather...

Soybean cultivation began in China more than 9 000 years ago. It has developed in Western countries in the early 20th century, and from the 1950s it started to become a huge industry in the United States.

Soybean is the most plant used the most as raw material: to make oil, soy and tamari sauces (soy sauce contain gluten while tamari doesn't), soy milk (tonyu), tofu, soy flour, soy germs, tempeh, miso…

But soybeans are also produced to feed animals: the two third of US soybeans are actually used for this purpose, which represent half of the total worldwide production of soybeans.

Soybean is also used in multiple industrial non-food applications such as fuel, plastics, adhesives, paint, or printing inks.

Leaky gut syndrome (LGS, also called "increased intestinal permeability") is a digestive condition that affects the lining of the intestines, making it too porous and even creating large cracks or holes. Those gaps allow bacteria and other toxic substances to pass through and escape into the bloodstream.

Researchers have found significant evidence regarding leaky gut causes and symptoms, yet there is still a lot to discover.

Gluten, gut bacteria imbalance, medications, chronic stress, processed foods and alcohol may contribute to leaky gut. Its symptoms can be various: skin problems (eczema, dermatitis), brain fog, chronic fatigue, food sensitivities, and even celiac disease, inflammatory bowel syndrome, or lupus.

The cook Marie-Antoine (Antonin by his nickname) Carême has, in 1821, invented the chef's hat. Other forms of headgear already existed at the time, but they were mismatched and, according to him, messy in the kitchen. He decided it would be of white color (sign of cleanliness in the kitchen), and he imposed different heights of caps according to the rank, the Chef wearing the highest hat.

Carême opened his own pastry shop at the age of 18 while continuing his training with the greatest cooks, he published numerous books which had become bestsellers, and was the first chef to call himself "chef". A nice revenge on life as he came from an extremely poor family in a sibling group of 14 children.

Edible marine algae (also called "sea vegetables") are classified according to their color: green, brown and red.

If some algae have a protein content of up to 50%, the digestibility of the latter is relatively low. They are however rich in minerals, vitamins and fibers.

In Western countries, most people don't have the habit to consume seaweed, but it has always been eaten in some Asian countries such as Japan, Korea, or China. The most popular seaweed in the world is wakame, also known as sea fern: this brown seaweed can be eaten fresh or dried and is appreciated for its texture, its slight iodized taste and its nutritional composition. The best known algae is undoubtedly the Nori seaweed, used to make sushi.

The first school canteen opened in France in 1844, shortly after the laws making school compulsory. Émile Depasse, mayor of Lannion, took this measure to fight poverty in his commune. This initiative was then copied across the country, still supported by town halls. Many years later, in 1936, the construction or fitting out of a refectory in each school became compulsory in France.

Nowadays, Korea is one of the countries where children eat the most balanced meals in canteens; moreover their meals are entirely free. At the other end, American children often eat too much fatty, sweet and salty food in US canteens, and have only 30 minutes to eat and relax.

The term "cacao" refers to the plant or its beans before processing, while the term "chocolate" (coming from the Aztec word "xocoatl") refers to anything made from the beans.

Chocolate was discovered in Mexico in 1527 by Cortés, and arrived in Europe in the 1610s. Nowadays, roughly two-thirds of the world's cocoa is produced in Western Africa, Côte d'Ivoire being the leading cocoa producing country.

Cocoa is rich in magnesium (300mg per 100g of food), but most modern chocolate being highly-refined and mass-produced, watch out for added sugar and fat: 25g of dark chocolate contains 1.5 pieces of sugar, and 25g of milk (or white) chocolate contains 3 pieces of sugar.

An oil is a fatty substance which is fluid at room temperature. It can be made from fruit (olive, nuts, hazelnut, almond, coconut), seeds (rapeseed, peanut, soy, sunflower), germ (wheat, corn) or seeds (grapes, squash).

If all oils contain 99.9% lipids, they are very different in their nutritional composition:
- The oils with the highest levels of saturated fats (which are to be avoided) are coconut and palm oils.
- Poly-unsaturated oils are rich in omega-3 and omega-6. Omega 3- are found in linseed, nut, rapeseed and soybean oils while omega-6 are in sunflower, soya, and sesame.
- Oils containing the most mono-unsaturated fats are olive and peanut oils.

Several thousands of different plant species have been used in the history of human nutrition; nowadays, we only cultivate 150 of them. Nowadays, 75% of human energy needs come from only 9 plants (wheat, rice, corn, barley, sorghum, potato, sweet potato, sugar cane, soy) – of which 60% from 3 (rice, corn, wheat). In other words, 75% of the genetic diversity of cultivated plants has been lost in a century. Some have been destroyed by pollution, disease, global warming; others have been abandoned in favor of standardized agriculture.

The phenomenon also exists in the animal kingdom. In Europe, half of the breeds have been eradicated since the start of the century, and a third of the remaining 770 breeds are at risk.

The Michelin Guide, also known as the Red Guide, was created in 1900 by André Michelin and his brother Édouard, owners of the tire company called Michelin. It was at first an advertising guide offered with the purchase of tires.

The guide then included advertisements and announcements of diverse hotels and mechanics; the suppression of advertisements was solemnly announced in 1908. A few years later, in 1920, the Michelin Guide stopped being given for free.

In order to distinguish the best restaurants, the 1st star was created in 1926; then appeared in 1930 the 2nd and the 3rd stars.

In the past few years, the guide also started to rate street food places!

In butchery, there are 3 different categories according to the parts of the animal. To each corresponds the ideal type of cooking:

- For posterior parts (thighs) and back (lumbar), a rapid cooking such as grilled, sautéed and roasted is recommended.
- For anterior parts (shoulders) and coastal regions, it is better to use a longer cooking method such as pan-fried, braised and sautéed.
- As for collar, abdominal muscles, chest, and outside of the limbs, a very long cooking such as poached and in sauce is required.

However, more than half of the world's beef sold today is minced steak, the latter only being created in 1940!

Icing sugar – also called powdered sugar or confectioners' sugar – became essential in cuisine (mainly in pastry) from the 18th century. For its ability to easily dissolve in water, it also comes handy while preparing juices, milkshakes or any cold beverages.

It is obtained by grinding and sieving the crystallized sugar until its crystals are smaller than 0.15 millimeters in size, and therefore form an intangible very fine powder. Starchy materials are then added to the powder to prevent caking and clumping before of air humidity.

Starchy materials, as its name suggests, contain starch. They are not negligible since they represent approximately 2 to 3% of the final product: be careful therefore in case of gluten intolerance.

If you kept a bite of white bread in your mouth for a long period of time, it would start to get really mushy, then to taste sweet. The reason is there are enzymes in the saliva, which break down the complex carbohydrates in the bread into simple sugars.

Enzymes are biological molecules that exist in the human body and that are vital for life. To date, approximately 75,000 enzymes are thought to exist and are divided into 3 classes according to their role:

- Metabolic enzymes run our bodies.
- Digestive enzymes digest our food.
- Food enzymes from raw foods start our food digestion.

Examples of digestive enzymes are amylase, pepsin and trypsin.

Nowadays, it is estimated that more than 25 million dogs are eaten each year worldwide. The main consumer countries are China, South Korea and Indonesia. Beside, a festival is held each year in Yulin, Guangxi, China in which various dog meat dishes are eaten. Between 10,000 and 15,000 dogs are estimated to be killed for this festival each year.

The highest rabbit meat consumption per capita is in Western Europe with 1.7kg of rabbit meat per inhabitant per year.

Hippophagy is the consumption of horse meat. If it is taboo in France and in Anglo-Saxon countries, some countries such as Russia, Kyrgyzstan, Kazakhstan, China, Japan, Mexico and Italy traditionally eat it.

Napoleon hated wasting time at the table and spent no more than 15 minutes there. Yet today, French people are the champions of time spent at the table: on average 2h13 per day. This is slightly more than the Spanish, Greek, Italian and Danish (around 2 hours), which complete the top-5.

At the other end are the Americans and Canadians who spent at table half the time of French people (1h02). Chinese (1h36), Australians (1h31), Indians (1h19) and Englishmen (1h18) are in between.

While 20 years ago the French lunch break was around 1h30, it is 50 minutes today. It's slightly more than 45 minutes for the Italians while Englishmen, Americans and Dutchmen spend only between 10 and 30 minutes for their lunch.

Instant coffee, also known as soluble coffee, coffee crystals, and coffee powder, was invented in 1890 by the New Zealander David Strange.

The technique used to make it is called lyophilization or atomization. It consists in reducing the water content, which prevents micro-organisms from growing, and therefore increases the shelf life of the product. On the other hand, not only does this technique destroy vitamins that are not heat-resistant, it also increases the food glycemic index and alters its organoleptic qualities.

This process is used today for many other products: dehydrated soups, infant milks, aromatic herbs, dehydrated mushrooms, cubed broths, cereals...

Insect farming can be done for various purposes: consumption of course, but also scientific study, harvesting of silk or honey or even the fight against crop pests. There are 2,000 species of edible insects such as grasshoppers, caterpillars, beetles, bees, ants, wasps, crickets and crickets.

If the West world is largely resistant to the idea of eating insects, some countries in Africa, Asia and Central America have always consumed them. Thailand is both the world's largest producer and consumer of insects.

Insects are an excellent source of protein (for example 69% in crickets while 25% in beef) and they supply all 9 essential amino acids. Last but not least, their production is more ecological than meat or fish.

The food history began from the time hominids first appeared. The standing position freed the upper limbs, which enabled them to use their hands for various activities, including feeding.

Homo sapiens, commonly known as "Modern Man" and appeared around 200,000 years ago, is a specie of primate belonging to the hominid family. At that time, he needed to eat the equivalent of 3,000 Calories per day, and was a hunter-gatherer: he fed on wild fruits and berries, he caught fish and hunted game. Vegetables represented more than two third of his diet.

Today, the daily Calories needed varies between 1800 and 2500 mainly depending on the sex, age, and activity.

Glycemic index (GI) describes the rate at which the body absorbs sugar. The slower it is, the more gradual the diffusion in the organism, which enables to have enough energy until the next meal without hunger. Foods with high GI on the opposite cause blood sugar spikes – which leads to pump ups and hunger.

The GI of a food is influenced by several factors: transformation process, starch type, fiber content, fruit maturity, lipid and acid content, preparation, degree of chewing of a food.

To simplify, foods are classified into 3 categories: low is below 50 (for example most green vegetables with a GI close to 15), moderate (like honey at 60), and high when above 65 (such as white flour at 85).

The first phytosanitary product was created in the 1890s to treat vine leaves against mildew: it is a mixture of copper sulphate and lime. Now they are today used in large quantities in various ranges of application – agriculture being the most important one.

The improvement of poison gas during the two world wars as well as the development of organic chemistry from the 1930s enabled a large number of synthetic pesticides to appear. For example, Agent Orange, a defoliant widely used by the United States military during the Vietnam War in the 1960s, or Glyphosate Roundup created in 1975. These two products were invented by Monsanto, a company bought in 2018 by the German pharmaceutical and agrochemical company Bayer.

Pasteurization, sterilization and canning are food conservation techniques which are not without consequences on health and taste aspects.

Pasteurization largely keeps both nutrients and organoleptic qualities of the products, but causes a large part of the heat-sensitive vitamins (in particular vitamin C) to be lost.

Sterilization and canning destroy all germs and toxins in the products, and greatly modify their nutritional values: heat-sensitive vitamins are destroyed, proteins are denatured, fibers are softened, water-soluble or liposoluble substances (depending on the type of covering liquid) are reduced, and sugar is hydrolyzed in acidic environment. In addition, color, texture and taste are largely modified.

Globally, more than 2 billion adults are overweight (30% of the total population) and 650 million are obese. Each year, over 3 million people die from the consequences of overweight or obesity.

The prevalence of obesity has tripled in the past 30 years. Researchers have estimated that if the eating habits do not change, 22% of the world's population will be obese in 2045 (compared to 14% in 2017).

The obesity rate has already reached 39% in the United States, and will increase to 55% if the Americans' eating habits do not change. This rate is around 30% in Australia, Mexico, the United Kingdom and Canada, 22% in Germany and Brazil, 15% in France… and only 6% in Singapore, 4% in Japan and 2% in Vietnam.

Contrary to what one might think, doctors' curriculum almost does not train in nutrition. The medical specialties are endocrinology, cardiology, gastroenterology, ophthalmology, pneumology, pediatrics, psychiatry, rheumatology, geriatrics… but dietetics is not one of them. Hippocrates would be crazy to hear that!

As a result, nowadays, the principles of modern medicine are very often a drug for each disease. More than $1.2 trillion has been spent on medicines last year, up from $887 billion in 2010. The United States is the largest consumer market in the world ($1,200 per person and per year), followed by Switzerland ($960/person), Canada ($830/person), Japan ($830/person), and Germany ($820/person).

Carbohydrates, proteins and fats provide the energy (measured in calories) that our bodies need to function properly. The amount of energy brought differs according to those nutrients since 1g of proteins or carbohydrates provides 4kcal and 1g of lipids brings 9kcal. As for alcohol, 1g provides 7kcalories.

These nutrients also differ in the speed at which the energy is released; for example, carbohydrates release it faster than fats.

These nutrients are digested the gastrointestinal tract (mouth, esophagus, stomach, small intestine, large intestine), where they get broken down into:
- Sugars for carbohydrates.
- Amino acids for proteins.
- Fatty acids and glycerol for lipids.

The first self-service grocery store was developed by entrepreneur Clarence Saunders in Memphis, Tennessee, United States. His first store opened in 1916 under the name Piggly Wiggly and were quickly developed in franchises.

In 1930, the first supermarket named King Kullen opened inside a 560m2 / 6,000-square-foot former garage in New-York city. This new type of store gained a lot of success thanks to the fact that consumers now had cars to reach the supermarket and do an abundant amount of grocery shopping, which could then be stored for long, thanks to refrigerators becoming more mainstream.

The first hypermarket appeared a few years later in Portland, Oregon: a combination of a supermarket, pharmacy and clothing shop.

An average American consumes more than 10kg of ice cream per year; New Zealand and Australia are completing the podium. There are several types of ice creams:

- Hard ice cream contains a mixture of cream and/or milk, sugar, fruit and/or flavoring, and sometimes eggs.
- Soft ice cream is made the same way, but frozen at a warmer temperature to preserve its silky-smooth consistency.
- Italian ice cream is dense and made with egg yolks, sugar, fruit and/or flavoring, and more milk than cream.
- Sorbet is a mixture of water, sugar and fruit (at least 35% of fruit).

In most industrial products, sugar is replaced by glucose syrup and there is no fruit.

North America's organic agricultural land is about 3.2 million hectares, which represents only 0.8% of the total agricultural area. In Austria, 23% of agricultural land is organic. Its principle is based on the non-use of GMOs, nor chemical and synthetic products (herbicides, preservatives); farmers use manure and compost.

Sustainable farming is another type of agriculture. It aims at optimizing economic results by using the least possible amount of pollutants. It still uses genetic selections of plants, fertilizers and artificial minerals.

Conventional agriculture (also known as intensive or industrial) refers to farming systems which include the use of phytosanitary products (fertilizers, pesticides, herbicides), GMO and machines.

In the 1990s, the mad cow scandal (BSE) made consumers aware that intensive production was not without risks. Since then however, food scandals have been repeated:
- 1999: chicken with dioxins.
- 2008: melamine in baby milk powder in China.
- 2011: listeriosis in the United States.
- 2011 : killing germinated seeds.
- 2012: IKEA tarts with feces.
- 2013: pure beef lasagna with horse (Spanghero / Findus).
- 2014: Taiwan Gutter Oil
- 2016: plastic in a Mars chocolate bar.
- 2017: Fipronil eggs contamination.
- 2017: Lactalis infant milk contaminated with Salmonella.

The term "vegan" was created in 1944 in London by Donald Watson, an English carpentry professor and animal rights advocate. He later founded the Vegan Society.

His initial purpose was to distinguish vegans from vegetarians — the vegan eating practice involving only foods from the plant world. It therefore excludes any product derived from animals, including their exploitation: leather, fur, wool, silk, beeswax, honey, gelatin, cosmetics and medicines tested on animals or containing animal substances.

This diet, which used to be followed by a very small minority of people, has nowadays gained much popularity, especially in Europe and the United States.

Minerals, vitamins and trace elements are necessary to be in good health:

- Minerals (also named mineral salts or macro-elements) are calcium, phosphorus, magnesium, sodium, and potassium. They are useful in large quantities.
- Trace elements are iron, iodine, selenium, fluorine, zinc, copper, manganese, chromium, and molybdenum. As its name suggests, required doses are most often very small.
- Vitamins can be water-soluble (soluble in water: vitamins B, C) or fat-soluble (soluble in fats: vitamins A, D, E and K, provitamin A). Recommended amounts depends on the nutrient itself.

Local sourcing and procurement has been for long the way to get access to products. In the Middle Ages, the fairground markets brought together producers and customers. Yet, the modernization of agriculture, the products standardization and the development of mass distribution (which has increased the number of intermediaries) have led to their decline in many countries.

In a context of food fears, they have actually experienced a revival since the 2000s. Nowadays, there are more and more farmers' markets in which food is directly sold by farmers to consumers, community-supported agriculture which enable growers and consumers to share both risks and benefits of food production, and food hubs that aggregate, distribute and market food from farmers to consumers.

Native from South America, tomatoes were introduced to Europe in the 16th century. Originally a tiny berry, European (especially Italian) gardeners have selected over generations the varieties that yield the most interesting fruits. Botanically, tomatoes are indeed fruits, although they are commonly used as a vegetable.

Tomatoes contain lycopene, a powerful antioxidant from the carotenoid family whose pigments are naturally red. In the late 1990s, tomato products' manufacturing multinationals (including Heinz) organized an awareness campaign to advertise its properties. Lycopene is also found in watermelon, papaya and pink grapefruit, and it is better absorbed by cooking and the presence of lipids.

The Coca-Cola drink has been inspired by a type of wine created in France in 1863. It was a preparation made from Peruvian coca leaves infused in Bordeaux wine, commonly known as "coca wine". Its inventor, the young pharmacy assistant Angelo François Mariani, marketed it under the name "Mariani wine".

From there in 1885, an American pharmacist created the "Pemberton's French Wine Cola", which was a non-alcoholic drink made from coca and cola nut. The following year, he slightly modified the recipe and changed its name to "Coca-Cola".

In 1904 cocaine was removed from the Coca-Cola, which recipe is still guarded trade secret today as a publicity, marketing and intellectual property protection strategy.

Infant formula, also called baby formula, baby milk or infant milk, was invented in 1860 in Switzerland by a pharmacist of German origin, named Henri Nestlé.

At the time, child malnutrition was significant and there was no alternative to breast milk. This innovation (a mixture of milk, flour, sugar and mineral salts) thus naturally and quickly spread in Switzerland after its launch in 1867, and then in the rest of Europe. From the 1870s, it was sold in Egypt, Russia, Mexico and Indonesia.

It makes sense to think baby food is very healthy. Yet in a study published in 2019, the WHO reported that out of 8,000 baby food products examined, almost a third contained added sugar or other sweeteners.

Ethylene is a gas naturally produced by various fruits, vegetables and flowers. Its particularity is to increase fruits and vegetables ripeness.

So, to ripen a plant more quickly at home, just place it in contact with a climacteric fruit (which produces a lot of this gas), such as passion fruit, apple, apricot, avocado, nectarine, pear, papaya, peach, tomato and onion. Overripe or rotten plants also produce high levels of ethylene.

On the other hand, some plants are sensitive to ethylene and ripen too quickly upon contact; this is the case of broccoli, lettuce, asparagus, potato, and carrot. Keep them away from your climacteric fruits!

A third of the world's population is likely to run out of water by 2025. While only 8% of the world's fresh water is used for domestic needs, agriculture consumes three-quarters of it. Some examples of the amount of water required for the production of:

- 1kg of beef: 14,500 liters.
- 1kg of pork, rice or cheese: approximately 5,000 liters of water.
- 1kg of chicken: 4000 liters of water.
- 1kg of eggs: 3,300 liters of water.
- 1kg of pasta: 1,700 liters of water.
- 1kg of soybeans: 900 liters of water.
- 1kg of potatoes, wheat, oranges or corn: between 500 and 600 liters of water.
- 1kg of tomatoes: 180 liters of water.
- 1L of beer : 25 liters of water.

Historically, it was thought that dairy products were essential to develop strong bones, but many studies claim nowadays the opposite.

In addition, if calcium is indeed good for bones, cow's milk (which contains 120mg of calcium per 100g) is far from being the biggest source: there are for example 400mg of calcium in 100g of sardines in oil, 350mg in 100g of tofu, 250mg in 100g of almonds, and 170mg in 100g of spinach.

While the consumption of dairy products worldwide is growing by 2.5% per year (mainly thanks to emerging countries), the Americans have reduced their consumption of dairy products by 37% and the French by 23% in the last 50 years.

The invention of the microwave oven only dates back to 1946 – 74 years ago. Engineer Percy Spencer, who overseen at that time a radar magnetron factory, realized that the chocolate bar he had in his pocket melted as he passed near a working magnetron.

How does it work? Short wave-length radiation called "microwaves" causes agitation of water molecules in food, which releases heat and cooks it.

From this discovery, the first microwave oven, called the Radarange, was designed and marketed. Yet not really the way you may imagine as it was rather different from current products: it measured almost two meters, weighted over three hundred kilos and costed several thousands of dollars!

Artificial meat, also called in vitro meat, is a laboratory meat produced from animal cells (not from traditional farming). The stem cells are immersed in a culture liquid containing amino acids, vitamins, sugar, growth hormones and fetal calf serum.

The first artificial steak was presented in August 2013 by Mark Post, a researcher at the University of Maastricht, and was called the "Frankenburger". Since then, many laboratories and researchers have worked on developing the artificial steak that would taste the closest to farming-meat taste.

If it is still too expensive to market it today, their cost has already considerably dropped: from €250,000 for a 150g steak in 2013 to less than €50 today.

Besides its gastronomic interest, garlic has exceptional therapeutic properties; however, it also causes persistent unpleasant breath!

It is only after being cut that garlic develops its aroma. The molecule responsible for the unpleasant breath is called allyl methyl sulfide. Once the garlic has been digested, it ends up in the bloodstream and is then transported to the lungs to be exhaled with exhalation, making toothbrushing rather ineffective.

On the other hand, certain polyphenols (antioxidants) enable to decrease it. They are found for example in parsley, mint and spinach, but also in lemon juice, green tea and, especially, in apples (in particular if eaten raw).

There are two types of diabetes. Type-1, which affects between 5 and 10% of the diabetics, is due to an absence of insulin secretion by the pancreas. The 90-95% others suffer from type-2 diabetes. Linked to improper use of insulin by the body's cells, type 2 diabetes is characterized by chronically high blood sugar and comes from a diet that is too rich in sugar. It can thus be reversed with healthy lifestyle decisions.

In the United States, 75% of food contains added sugars, more than one in three American adults have become resistant to insulin (it's one in ten globally, which is twice more than 30 years ago), and around 30 million Americans have diabetes. Throughout the world, 1 out of 3 adults has prediabetes; of this group, 9 out of 10 don't know they have it.

Flavorings are present in many food products to change or adapt their flavor (taste and smell). If we know there are natural and artificial flavorings, it is less commonly spread that natural flavors can actually also be... artificial!

The regulations call "natural flavoring" a flavor that exists in nature. It can be extracted directly from the plant or animal raw materials, or synthesized (artificial natural flavor).

For example, a natural vanilla flavor can come from vanilla, vanillin found in beet pulp, or even be made from ferulic acid from rice bran or pulp. Only the mention "natural vanilla flavoring" will ensure you consume vanilla.

Proteins are made up of amino acids. Our body needs 20 types of amino acids to function properly, and is able to synthesize 11 of them; the other 9 (called essential amino acids) must be provided by food.

Animal proteins, quinoa and buckwheat contain these 9 essential amino acids: they are what is named "complete proteins".

Yet, one can be in good health without eating this food. A varied plant-based diet provides all amino acids necessary to our body since some of them are deficient in certain amino acids but in excess in another one. For example, cereals and legumes are complementary: cereals contain in excess the essential amino acid "methionine" and have the limiting amino acid "lysine"; the opposite is true for legumes.

Gluten, from the Latin "glu" (glue), is a very elastic and viscous protein whose volume increases considerably during cooking. The more it is folded on itself, the more it hardens; thus it gives substance to the dough and enables the ingredients to bond well together.

The main gluten-containing grains are wheat, rye, barley, spelt and oat. There is no gluten is grains such as buckwheat, corn, quinoa, chestnut, rice, millet, potato, and cassava.

Celiac disease is a chronic disease of the intestine triggered by the consumption of gluten. It is principally manifested by digestive symptoms such as diarrhea, pain, or bloating, and it has an inherited component.

Food classification based on carbohydrate, fat and protein levels began around 1870.

As for the notion of "calorie", it was defined by the chemist and physicist Nicolas Clément in 1824, then adapted to food around 1880. Scientifically speaking, 1,000 calories is the amount of heat needed to raise the temperature of 1kg of water by 1°C (33.8°F).

In addition, one should not confuse a calorie with a Calorie. 1 Calorie is equivalent to 1 kilocalorie (1 kcal, as indicated on the labels of food products which thus mean 1,000 calories). Calorie and calorie being identical when we speak, we largely use today the word calorie to speak in reality of Calorie — that is to say kilocalorie (kcal).

French people are the biggest cheese eaters in the world (23kg per person each year). More than 1,000 different varieties are produced there, classified into 8 families:

- Cooked pressed cheese (comté).
- Uncooked pressed cheese (tomme).
- Blue-veined cheese (roquefort).
- Soft rind-washed cheese (livarot).
- Soft cheese with a bloomy rind (camembert).
- Goat cheese (chabichou).
- Fresh cheeses (petits suisses).
- Processed cheeses (mixtures of cheeses and butter, cream, or milk).

Nowadays, only 5% of Camembert sold worldwide are made from raw milk; the rest is made from thermized, sterilized, or artificially cultured milk.

Ortho-molecular medicine uses the nutrients and substances (vitamins, enzymes, minerals, hormones, amino acids) naturally known by the body to prevent and treat certain disorders and maintain health. It was practiced without having a name long ago, yet healing food has lost ground to modern surgery when the latter became more advanced.

Linus Pauling, Nobel Prize in chemistry, created this term in 1968. Ortho-molecular means "correct molecule" in the sense "which is not foreign to the human body, which is biologically correct"; the other molecules (the active ingredients in most medicines) are seen as biologically incorrect because they are unnatural for humans.

In 2016, Walmart (hypermarkets global giant) filed a patent which seeks to developing autonomous robot bees: equipped with camera and sensors, these flying mini-drones would spot flowers, collect pollen and transport it. This is still an embryonic project and these bee robots do not yet exist, but many researchers are working on it.

While 75% of world food production depends on bees, we are facing with the collapse of its population (each year in France, nearly 30% of bee colonies disappear due to intensive agriculture and pesticides). Consequently, many other projects have emerged such as the RoboBees (Harvard University, United States) or the Japanese pollinator robots.

It was under Napoleon in the 1810s that a cost-effective process for producing sugar from beets was developed. It was previously only used to feed animals.

If 124 countries produce sugar, Brazil and India are the biggest producing countries, counting for more than the third of global production (around 63 million metric tons over the 180 produced worldwide). The three quarters of sugar production is sugarcane, and most of the remaining is derived from sugar beet.

Whether from beets or cane, sugar contains 99.9% simple carbohydrates. White and brown sugars are nutritionally equivalent, there are just more impurities in brown sugar, which very slightly decreases the carbohydrate content.

Iron, one of the main components of hemoglobin, is an essential mineral for the proper oxygenation of our tissues and cells. When a person is deficient in iron, its issues and muscles won't get enough oxygen and be able to work effectively.

If we all know that there is iron in beef (2mg per 100g) and spinach (2.7mg per 100g), the mineral is found in much higher quantities in other food. It is for example the case of cumin (66mg per 100g), spirulina (29mg per 100g), sesame (17mg per 100g), soy (16mg per 100g), and cocoa (13mg per 100g).

Only 5 to 25% of the iron consumed is assimilated by our body. Non-heme iron (from plants and eggs) is better assimilated when consumed with vitamin C, for example citrus juice.

There are many types of eating disorders. Among the best known, bulimia is characterized by crisis in which a person excessively ingests food without being able to stop, then makes him/herself vomit.

The anorexic person, on the other hand, in his/her fear of becoming fat or gaining weight, fights hard against any weight gain, which results in obstinate food restriction and vomiting.

A less known disease named orthorexia is the obsession of healthy eating and the systematic rejection of foods perceived as unhealthy. Another type of eating disorder is hyperphagia, or overeating, and consists of eating compulsively and without hunger until you feel pain in the stomach, but without vomiting or taking laxatives.

Until the end of the 18th century, food was preserved thanks to salt, smoking, vinification, fermentation, alcohol, vinegar, fat or even sugar. These traditional processes enable a better preservation of food thanks to the lowering of water activity, the lowering of pH (most bacteria do not develop at an acidic pH) or, in the case of alcohol, by an antiseptic effect.

These methods, however, only partially preserve; plus they distort the initial organoleptic qualities of the products. Many techniques were then invented with the aim to preserve for longer and keep as much as possible the initial organoleptic properties of the food: caning, sterilization, freezing, or even ionization. Yet none of those techniques keeps intact the food nutritional proprieties.

The "roux", which is today the basis for countless sauces, was invented in 1650 by Pierre de La Varenne, a French cook. It is a mixture of fat and flour in equal amounts, which is called " tant pour tant." Fat can be butter, clarified butter, poultry fat or oil, butter being the classic ingredient. Once the roux is cooked (on low heat), a liquid (milk, broth or stock) is added, its type and quantity being different depending on the use.

"White roux" (also called "velouté") is the basis of most white sauces as well as bechamel sauce. The "blond roux" is cooked longer until it turns blond in color. Lastly, the "brown roux" (which is the base of brown sauces) is cooked until reaching an amber color.

Originally, the French service is what we now call a buffet: the guests are standing and serving themselves on a table containing the dishes. Today, the French-style service consists of bringing the dishes ordered to the table, then the guests serve themselves: as it enables a friendly atmosphere, it is often practiced in farmhouse inns.

In English and Russian service, the waiter brings the dishes to the dining room, presents them to customers, starting with the women, and then serves them. This type of service is used today to draw attention on some dishes such as flambé dishes or the preparation of a prime rib.

The plate service is the most used today: the plates are prepared in the kitchen and brought to the guests.

World Vegetarian Day takes place annually on October 1st. The day brings global attention to the health and environmental benefits of vegetarianism, and focuses on the ethics of following a vegetarian lifestyle. World Vegetarian Day was founded in 1977 by the North American Vegetarian Society (NAVS), and was endorsed by the International Vegetarian Union in 1978.

World Vegan Day is an annual event celebrated by vegans around the world every 1st November.

It is in Israel, and more precisely in Tel Aviv, that the world's largest vegan festival was held: the Vegan Fest. The first edition took place in 2014 and attracted more than 10,000 visitors, the second took place in 2019.

Food poisoning is an infection or disruption of the body after eating food contaminated with a bacteria, a virus or a parasite.

It can be linked to the ingestion of a fresh food that has not been washed or washed with contaminated water, a food that is poorly preserved or whose cold chain has not been respected, or even a bad food or uncooked.

If food poisoning is generally mild and goes away on its own, it can be dangerous and lead to death. An estimated 600 million – almost 1 in 10 people in the world – fall ill after eating contaminated food and 420 000 die every year. Diarrhoeal diseases are the most common illnesses resulting from the consumption of contaminated food.

The acidity of a large part of red fruits (currants, raspberries, blackberries…) comes from anthocyanins. Anthocyanin is an antioxidant of purple, blue or red color, and is found in skin of the fruits.

The purple reddish color of beets is not related to anthocyanins but to betanin, another pigment having antioxidant effects too. Betanin is also found in pitayas (dragon fruit) with red flesh.

Since the pigments (and thus the antioxidants) are mainly present in the skin of fruits and vegetables, the latter have fewer nutrients (vitamins, minerals and fibers) when they are eaten peeled. However, peeling them eliminates toxic residues that are also mainly present on the skin (nitrate, pesticides…).

Traditional medicine, sometimes called "complementary", "alternative", " integrated" or "unconventional" medicine, has been practiced for thousands of years. Millions of people use it around the world today; in some Asian and African countries, 80% of the population actually depends on it for primary health care (especially herbal treatments). Since 1990, it has become popular again in many countries both developed and developing.

There are different types of traditional medicine such as Chinese medicine, Ayurveda (originally from India), acupuncture, homeopathy, or naturopathy. The International Classification of Diseases published by WHO in 2018 includes a new chapter on traditional medicine.

Food can be preserved thanks to several heat techniques:

- Pasteurization: 30 minutes at 64°C/147°F (low pasteurization), a few minutes at 80°C/178°F (high pasteurization), or a few seconds at 95°C/203°F (flash pasteurization). Pasteurized products must be kept at refrigerated temperature.
- Sterilization: 15 minutes at 120°C/248°F (standard sterilization), or a few seconds at 145°C/292°F (Ultra High Temperature). They can be stored at room temperature
- Canning: two heat treatments, first above 60°C/140°F, then above 115°C/239°F. They can be stored at room temperature.

Starch is a white substance coming either from cereal seeds (corn, wheat, rice) or from certain tubers, rhizomes, roots or stems of plants (potato, cassava, tapioca, sago, sweet potato...). It is tasteless and odorless and is made by removing the protein and fiber of the cereal, leaving only the starchy part. Very refined, the starch is basically one step away from being a sugar.

If starch is heated in a liquid, the solution thickens. This is why it is used in cooking as a binder, to give a creamy consistency and transform a liquid into a soup, a sauce or a cream.

The starch also makes the cakes lighter (as it doesn't contain any protein), but be careful not to replace all the flour by starch, otherwise the cake will crumble.

Food additives are substances not consumed as food per se, and added to food products to keep or improve their freshness (preservation), their taste (aroma), their texture (to thicken, to prevent from foaming, from gluing), their appearance (color, to make it shine), their nutritional qualities (reduce calories).

These additives often appear in the ingredients of the food packaging made in Europe with the letter E followed by three numbers. The figure just after the E corresponds to the additive function (for example, 1 stands for colorants, 2 for preservatives, 3 for the antioxidants, 6 for the flavor enhancers, 7 for the antibiotics..). More than 300 additives are now authorized in Europe.

A genetically modified organism (also called transgenic) has a modified DNA through genetic engineering. In most cases, they have been altered with DNA from another organism (bacterium, plant, virus or animal).

The most widely cultivated genetically modified plant species are soybeans and maize, which occupy more than 81% of the cultivated area of GMOs. Rice, papaya, eggplant, potato or beetroot are also regularly subject to genetic modification.

Main producers are the United States (75 millions of hectares), Brazil (50 millions), Argentina (24 millions), Canada (13 millions), and India (12 millions).

78% of soybeans grown worldwide are transgenic. Over 90% of American soybeans and corn are genetically modified.

The body's oxidation process produces free radicals, which are unstable substances whose production increases in the presence of processed foods, UV exposure, pollution, smoke, alcohol, lack of sleep, chemical products, and stress. When the body can no longer eliminate these free radicals effectively, an oxidative stress occur, which is linked to many diseases such as cardiovascular disease and some cancers.

Antioxidants neutralize these free radicals. There are several hundreds (or even thousands) of substances with an antioxidant effect: vitamins C and E, polyphenols, lycopene, and tannins — to name a few. The best sources are found in fruits, vegetables and certain oils. Each antioxidant having a different role, it is necessary to have a varied diet.

Animal fats have long been used in cooking. Lard (pork fat) is mainly used in cold meats, pâtés, rillettes, biscuits and low-fat products. Tallow (beef and mutton fat) is barely used today. Poultry fat (goose and duck) is still commonly used in the Southwest part of France for the regional cuisine (where foie gras comes from).

If all these types of fats contain 99.5% lipids, and therefore provide around 9kcal per 100g, their nutritional profiles differ; they are therefore more or less good for health. For example, poultry fat provides 30% of saturated fatty acids while it is more than 50% in mammal fat. Saturated fats should be limited to less than 5 to 8% of the total daily calorie intake according to The American Heart Association and the World Health Organization.

Glutamate is an amino acid found naturally in our bodies, and in foods like mushrooms, tomatoes and grapes. It is a neurotransmitter that plays a key role in the learning and the memory process.

It is also a chemical additive (E621) widely used in the food industry as a flavor enhancer in the form of monosodium glutamate (also called MSG). 1,500,000 tons of glutamate is estimated to be produced each year worldwide.

These substance provide an umami flavor which is considered by Japanese people to be the 7th flavor (after sweet, salty, bitter, acid, astringent, and spicy). Yet, it is a highly addictive substance that acts like a drug on the brain.

A tomato produced in Germany in March contains 12mg of vitamin C compared to 25mg if produced in August. Tomatoes need heat, humidity and light to be fully ripe, and therefore to be highly concentrated in nutrients. This common sense rule applies to all plants.

Glasshouse forcing does not enable the fruits and vegetables to synthesize the constituents in a normal way, which gives a strong advantage to seasonal vegetal.

In addition, seasonal fruits and vegetables have more taste, contain less pesticides and are less expensive. Furthermore, consuming seasonal vegetal promotes the economic and sustainable development of local production.

The term "wheat" has long been used to refer to all grains. It is a word which today includes cereals of the "Triticum" type. While 2,400 varieties of wheat are listed in the European Catalog, two types of wheat cultivation dominate today.

Soft wheat (also called white wheat) comes from culture crossing and is by far the most cultivated. Characterized by a high protein and gluten content, its flour is perfect to make breads, pancakes, cookies, pastries, or even pizzas.

Durum wheat (often called pasta wheat) is known for its hardness, its high protein content, its yellow color and its cooking qualities. Representing 4% of world wheat production, it is essentially used for the production of pasta and couscous.

Hard meat is often linked to animal stress. Stress causes the production of hormones resulting in muscle hyper-contraction.

Meat aging is also very important to have a tender, juicy meat with good organoleptic quality. This natural process (called staling) takes place in a cold room for 1 to 8 weeks on the entire parts of the animal.

In order to have tender meat, it must be removed from the refrigerator 20 to 30 minutes before cooking. The fact the meat goes back to ambient temperature enables to avoid the "aggression" of the thermal shock caused by cooking.

However, a good meat is first and foremost animals raised slowly and pastured on grass in traditional farming.

The fork arrived in Italy at the end of the Middle Ages, and then spread to the rest of Europe.

It became common in Europe in the 16th century because at that time it was no longer tolerable to take food where others have put their hands. It is in Europe and in Northern America that the fork is the most used today.

Nowadays, 3.5 billion people eat with their fingers (fingers alone or with utensils such as a spoon), mainly in Asia and Africa. The right hand is often used, the left hand being considered unclean in many religions and traditions.

2.1 billion people eat with chopsticks, mainly in Asia and in particular in China.

India is (by far) the country with the largest share of vegetarians in its population: almost 40%. Israel and Taiwan complete the podium (13%). In Israel, vegetarianism is linked to Judaism, a religion which recommends to limit meat consumption. In Taiwan, the government is encouraging people to eat less meat.

About 10% of the English population is vegetarian; it's 9% in Italy, Germany and Austria, 7% in the United States, 4% in Canada, and only 2% in France. There, a new trend called "flexitarianism" has emerged: it is about eating less meat products without totally stopping it. French people have reduced their meat consumption by 15% between 2003 and 2015, and a third of them declare being flexitarians.

Fructose is the sugar found in fruit. It is to be distinguished from the industrially produced fructose, obtained by hydrolysis of corn, which is disastrous for health.

Also called "high fructose corn syrup", fructose syrup was invented in the United States in 1970. Apart from the fact that it contains no fiber nor vitamin, it is metabolized only by the liver and does not depend on insulin action; it therefore causes strong glycemic peaks which, if they are too regular, promote the storage of calories in fats.

It is found nowadays in most processed products: sodas, ice creams, dairy products, candies, sweet cookies and appetizers, breakfast cereals, fruit juices, chocolate bars, pizzas, or even surimi...

Chocolate is consumed worldwide today in very different forms... which were produced industrially over 100 years ago.

Chocolate powder has been invented by the Dutch Van Houten in 1828, by using a cocoa solubilization technique.

The first industrially produced hard chocolate bar (tablet) dates from 1836 and came out of a factory in Noisiel, France — from a company which later became Nestlé. This product was actually also the first industrially produced product.

With the aim to develop sales towards low wages workers, Philippe Suchard launched in 1901 the now famous Suchard individually wrapped chocolates. The first chocolate bar (candy bar) was then launched in Chicago in 1923 by Franck Mars.

Fermentation is the natural transformation of carbohydrates into acids, gases or alcohols under the action of yeasts, bacteria or molds. Fermentation helps make food more digestible, nutritious and flavorful. There are actually different types of fermentations, with two main ones.

Alcoholic fermentation is carried out using brewer's or baker's yeast to make wine, beer, or even bread.

Lactic acid fermentation acts thanks to lactobacilli. Known to boost our intestinal flora, it can be used to make sauerkraut, pickles, dairy products, sourdough bread or tempeh, to name a few.

The acetic fermentation is used to make vinegar, and the propionic fermentation to make hard pressed cheese like Emmental.

Natural vitamin E − which is found for example in almonds, olive oil, sunflower seeds and fatty fish −, is 2 to 3 times more active in our body and better assimilated than synthetic vitamins. This is also the case with other vitamins.

If synthetic molecules almost have the same shape as natural molecules, they actually deflect light differently. This is because of their spatial conformation (they are said to be levogyres or dextrogyres). This fact makes them much less assimilable by the organism.

The good news is that it is quite easy to know if our food products and food supplements contain natural or synthetic vitamins: everything that does not have the mention "natural" is synthetic!

Honey is the only food with an eternal shelf life. Honeys are sold according to their geographical origin and the flower foraged by the bees. There are poly-floral honeys (bees have gathered honey from all types of flowers) and mono-floral honeys (either acacia, or lavender, or another flower).

Honey is produced from the nectar of flowers sucked in by bees and then deposited in their hive thanks to two phenomena:

- An enzyme found in the saliva of foraging bees converts sucrose into glucose-fructose.
- The flapping of the bees' wings lowers the humidity of the nectar.

It takes about 5L of nectar to get 1L of honey. It contains 80% of simple sugars.

It is sometimes thought that alcohol warms the body. In reality, the feeling of warmth comes from the dilation of the blood vessels located on the surface of the skin, causing an influx of blood and giving this feeling of warmth.

But this warming of the surface of the skin takes place at the expense of the central temperature of the body which, on the other hand, cools (it decreases by half a degree for 50g of alcohol consumed). The feeling of warmth will disappear as soon as the blood vessels are no longer dilated.

In addition, alcohol dehydrates by urinating more by what is called osmosis (or the osmosis effect). It is this dehydration that actually causes the hangover effect after an excess.

Baker's yeast, used to raise bread dough, is a living being of the mushroom family. Those microorganisms consume the sugars in the dough and produce carbon dioxide, which bubbles and swells the preparation from the inside.

Baking powder is also used as a leavening agent. It contains an acid element (cream of tartar), a basic element (sodium bicarbonate) and a neutral element (cornstarch or potato starch). The mixture of acidic and basic components releases carbon dioxide in the form of gases remaining trapped in the dough. A spoon of bicarbonate can replace baking powder in a moist dough that requires cooking. The effects are enhanced if the preparation contains an acid element.

If it is largely known pasteurization was invented by Louis Pasteur in the 1860s, it is less spread that this technique was originally designed for wine.

The original goal was to prevent it from turning sour, and Pasteur had observed that wine spoilage decreased when it was heated to a certain temperature.

However, oenologists were very reluctant to apply this technique to wine. Since pasteurization eliminates all microorganisms, whether they are useful or harmful, this technique would prevent the wine from evolving. So oenologists and winemakers lobbied not to apply this technique to wine and were successful: it was thus applied to beer, and then to milk.

9 782957 137718